Classic Jazz Collection

27 jazz standards **newly** arranged for piano and voice

Amsco Publications
A Part of **The Music Sales Group**
New York/London/Paris/Sydney/Copenhagen/Berlin/Tokyo/Madrid

A note from the arranger:
These arrangements are all intermediate level.
The focus is on supporting the voice, so they're solid accompaniments with
the melody in the right hand, but have real jazz chord changes
reflecting the recordings I used.
I think it'll be a great collection with great titles.

Project editor: David Bradley
Arrangements by David Pearl

Order No. AM 987294
ISBN-13: 978-0-8256-3580-9

Exclusive Distributors:
Music Sales Corporation
257 Park Avenue South, New York, NY 10010 USA
Music Sales Limited
14-15 Berners Street, London W1T 3LJ England
Music Sales Pty. Limited
20 Resolution Drive, Caringbah, NSW 2229, Australia

Printed in the United States of America by
Vicks Lithograph and Printing Corporation

Contents

All Too Soon Ella **Fitzgerald** 4

Angel Eyes Frank **Sinatra** 7

April In Paris Count **Basie** 10

Ballerina Nat King **Cole** 16

Bewitched, Bothered and Bewildered Rosemary **Clooney** 20

Body And Soul Tony **Bennett** 13

Cheek To Cheek Fred **Astaire** 24

Crazy She Calls Me Rod **Stewart** 28

A Day In The Life Of A Fool Jack **Jones** 31

Everything Happens To Me Chet **Baker** 34

If You Could See Me Now Mel **Tormé** 42

In A Sentimental Mood Benny **Goodman** 45

It Don't Mean A Thing (If It Ain't Got That Swing) Louis **Armstrong** 48

I've Got You Under My Skin Michael **Bublé** 38

My Favorite Things Julie **Andrews** 52

My Funny Valentine Sarah **Vaughn** 56

A Night In Tunisia Dizzy **Gillespie** 60

Pennsylvania 6-5000 Glenn **Miller** 64

Prelude To A Kiss Nancy **Wilson** 76

Raindrops Keep Fallin' On My Head B.J. **Thomas** 68

'Round Midnight Miles **Davis** 72

Satin Doll Oscar **Peterson** 79

Someday My Prince Will Come Dave **Brubeck** 82

Sweet Georgia Brown Harry **Connick**, Jr. 84

Take The "A" Train Duke **Ellington** 87

There Is No Greater Love Amy **Winehouse** 90

Unforgettable Natalie **Cole** 94

All Too Soon

Words and Music by Carl Sigman and Duke Ellington

Angel Eyes

Words and Music by Matt Dennis and Earl Brent

April In Paris

Words by E.Y. Harburg
Music by Vernon Duke

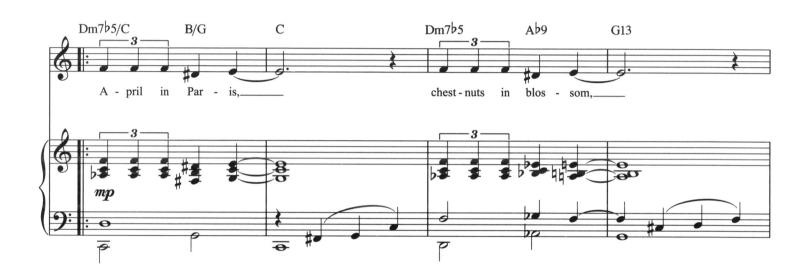

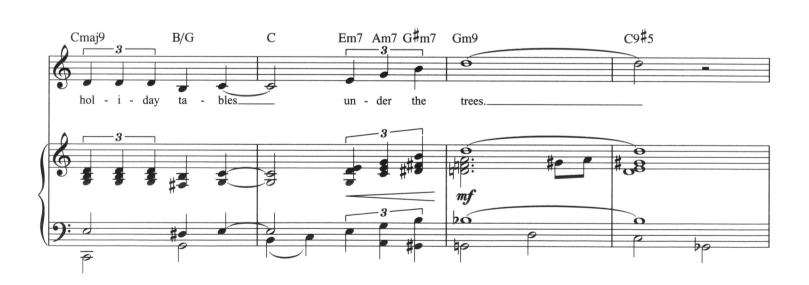

Body And Soul

Words by Edward Heyman, Robert Sour and Frank Eyton
Music by John Green

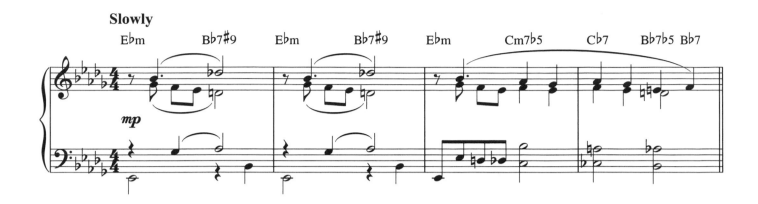

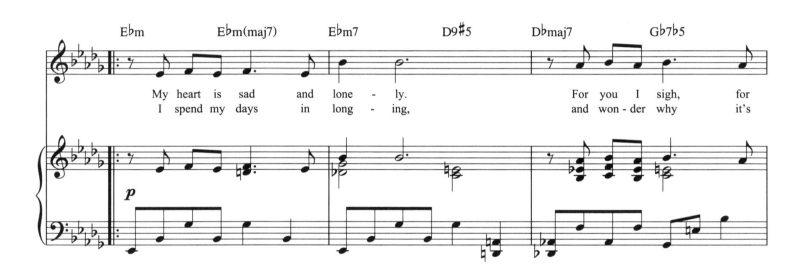

My heart is sad and lone - ly.
I spend my days in long - ing,

For you I sigh, for
and won - der why it's

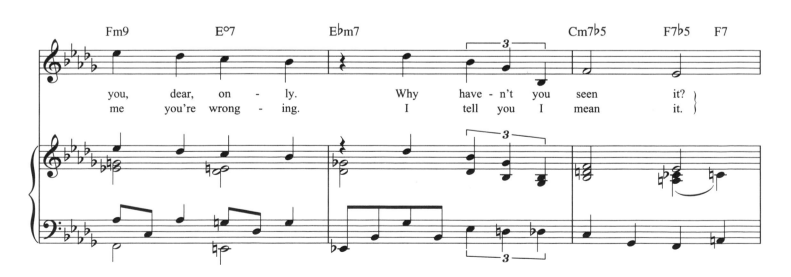

you, dear, on - ly.
me you're wrong - ing.

Why have - n't you seen it?
I tell you I mean it.

13

I'm all for you, bod-y and soul. soul.

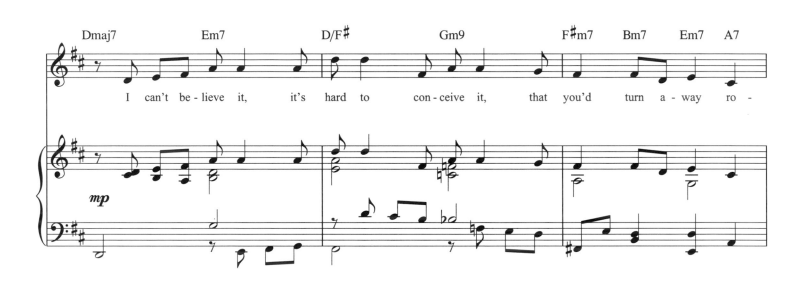

I can't be-lieve it, it's hard to con-ceive it, that you'd turn a-way ro-

mance. Are you pre-tend-ing? It looks like the end-ing, un-

less I could have one more chance to prove, dear. My life a wreck you're

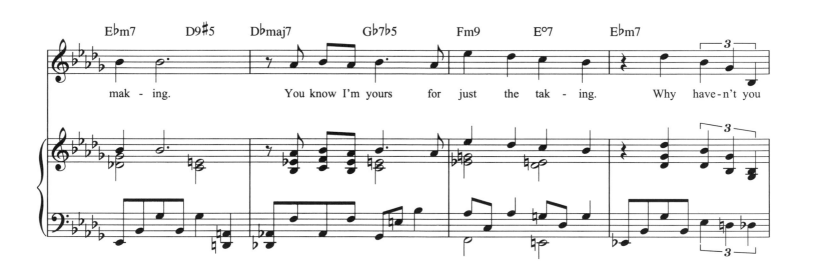

mak - ing. You know I'm yours for just the tak - ing. Why have-n't you

seen it? I'm all for you, bod - y and soul.

Ballerina

Words and Music by Carl Sigman and Bob Russell

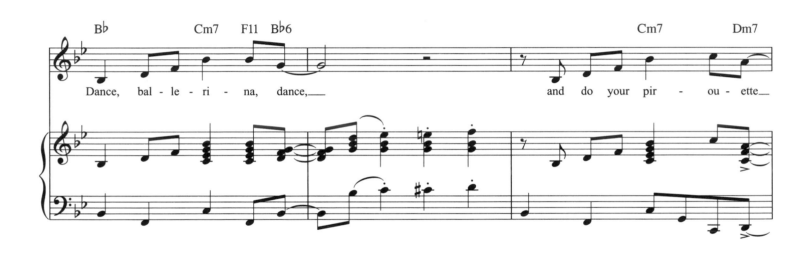

Bewitched, Bothered and Bewildered

(from *Pal Joey*)

Words by Lorenz Hart
Music by Richard Rodgers

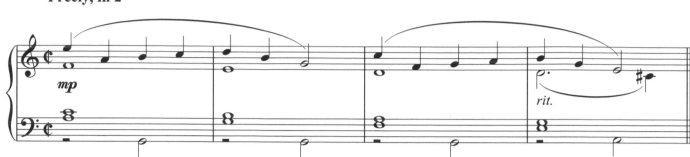

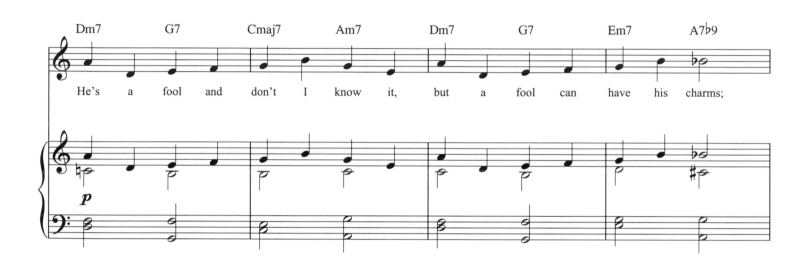

Cheek To Cheek

Words and Music by Irving Berlin

seem to find the hap - pi - ness I seek,____
van - ish like a gam - bler's luck - y streak,____
when we're

out to - geth - er danc-ing cheek to cheek.____

Oh, I love to climb a moun-tain and to
love to go out fish - ing in a

reach the high - est peak, but it does - n't thrill me half as much____ as
riv - er or a creek, but I don't en - joy it half as much____ as

Crazy She Calls Me

Words and Music by Carl Sigman and Bob Russell

A Day In The Life Of A Fool

English Lyric by Carl Sigman
Music by Luiz Bonfa

Everything Happens To Me

Words and Music by Matt Dennis and Tom Adair

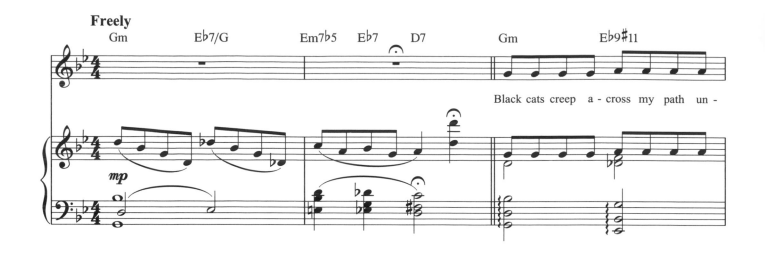

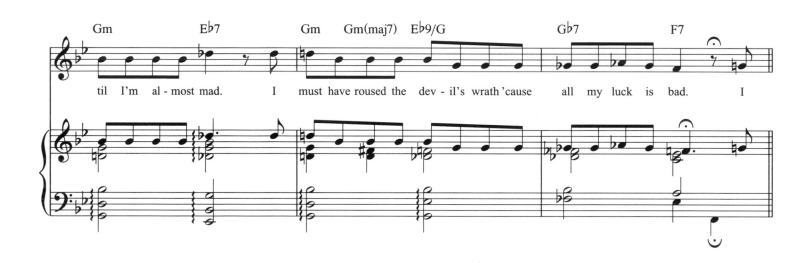

I've Got You Under My Skin

Words and Music by Cole Porter

Moderate Swing

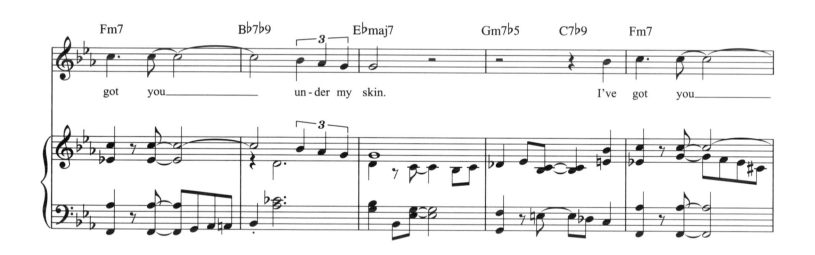

got you_____ un-der my skin. I've got you_____

—deep in the heart of me._____ So deep in my heart,_____ you're real-ly a

If You Could See Me Now

Words and Music by Carl Sigman and Tad Dameron

heart_____ be-hind the smile? The way I feel for you__ I nev - er could dis-guise.

The look of love is writ - ten plain - ly in my eyes. I think you'd be mine a - gain

if you could see me now._____ You'll

now._____

In A Sentimental Mood

Words and Music by Duke Ellington, Irving Mills and Manny Kurtz

It Don't Mean A Thing
(If It Ain't Got That Swing)

Words and Music by Duke Ellington and Irving Mills

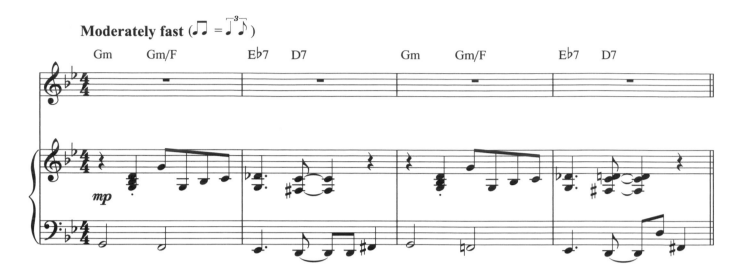

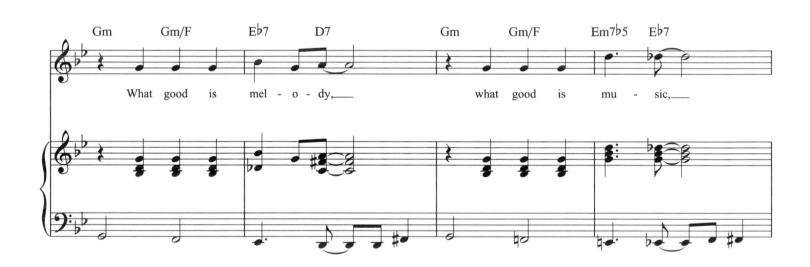

What good is mel-o-dy,___ what good is mu-sic,___

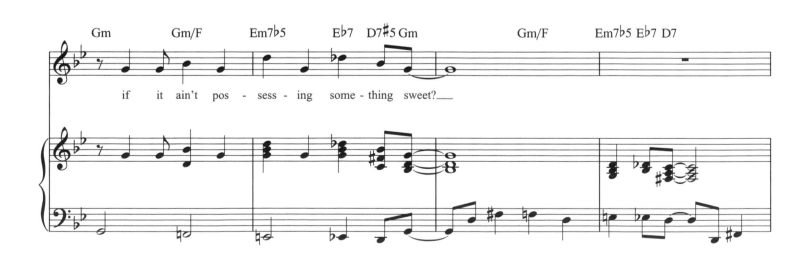

if it ain't pos-sess-ing some-thing sweet?___

It ain't the mel - o - dy,___ it ain't the mu - sic;___

there's some - thing else that makes the tune com - plete:___ It

don't mean a thing___ if it ain't got that swing.___

Doo wah,___ doo wah, doo wah, doo wah, doo wah,___ doo wah, doo wah, doo wah. It

49 It

My Favorite Things

(from *The Sound Of Music*)

Lyrics by Oscar Hammerstein II
Music by Richard Rodgers

Moderately bright Jazz Waltz

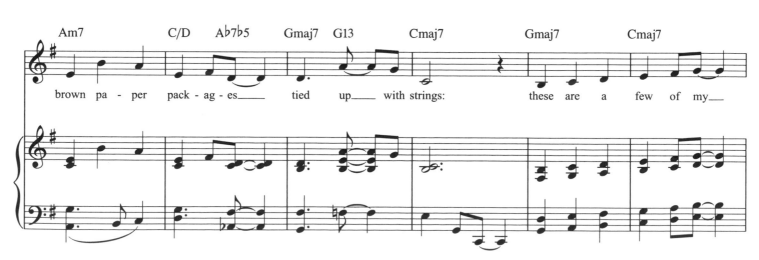

My Funny Valentine

(from *Babes In Arms*)

Words by Lorenz Hart
Music by Richard Rodgers

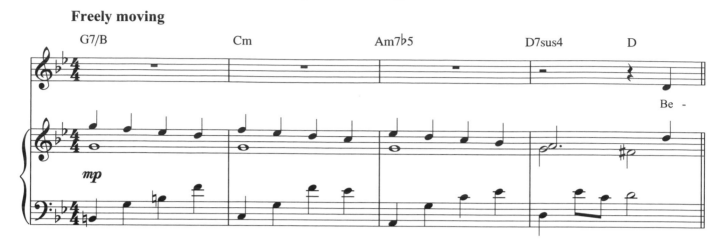

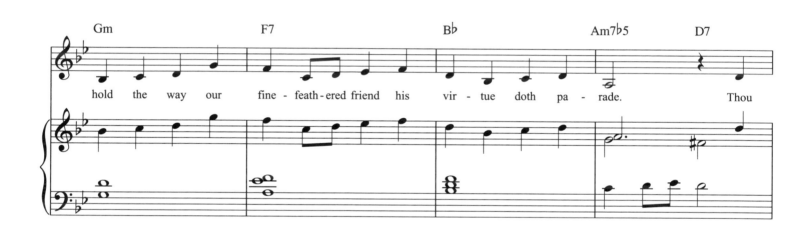

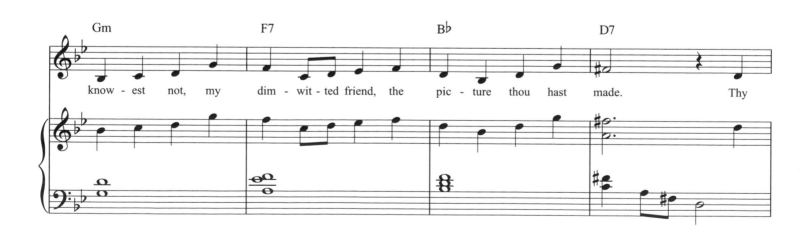

A Night In Tunisia

Words and Music by Dizzy Gillespie and Frank Paparelli

Moderately fast

Pennsylvania 6-5000

Words and Music by Carl Sigman, Jerry Gray and William J. Finegan

Raindrops Keep Fallin' On My Head

Words and Music by Burt Bacharach and Hal David

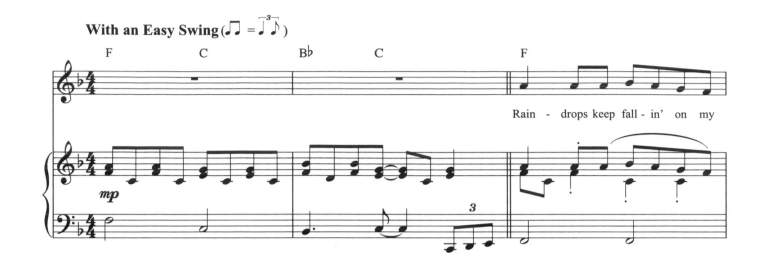

soon be turn - in' red. Cry - in's not for me 'cause

I'm nev - er gon - na stop the rain by com - plain - in.' Be - cause I'm

Faster

free, noth - in's wor - ry - in' me._____

rit.

(even 8th notes)

repeat and fade

'Round Midnight

Words by Bernie Hanighen
Music by Cootie Williams and Thelonious Monk

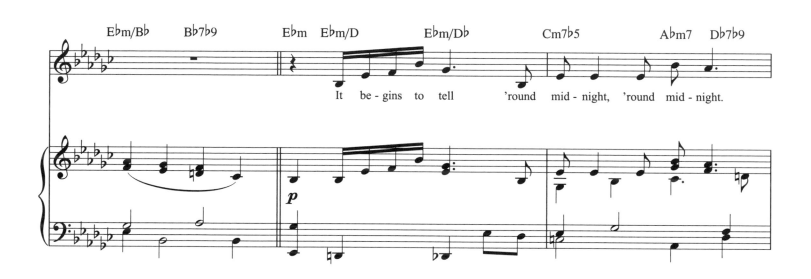

It be-gins to tell 'round mid-night, 'round mid-night.

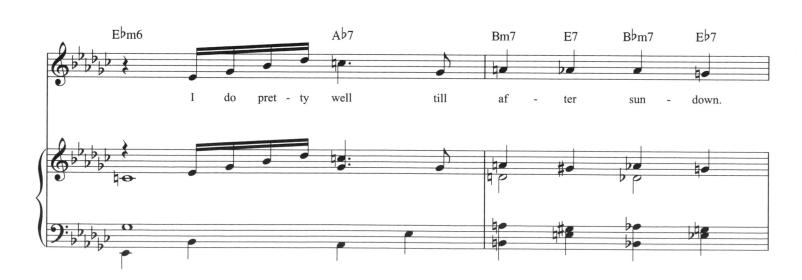

I do pret-ty well till af-ter sun-down.

Prelude To A Kiss

Words by Irving Gordon and Irving Mills
Music by Duke Ellington

Satin Doll

Words by Johnny Mercer and Billy Strayhorn
Music by Duke Ellington

Someday My Prince Will Come

Words by Larry Morey
Music by Frank Churchill

Moderate Jazz Waltz

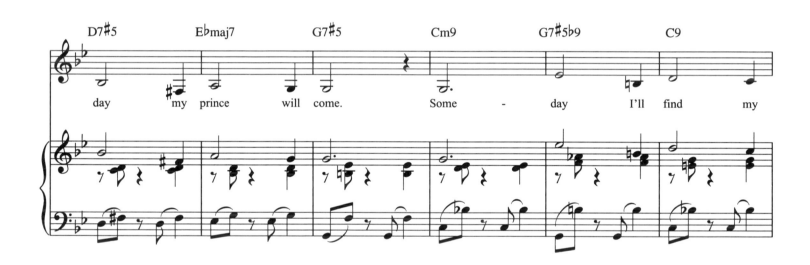

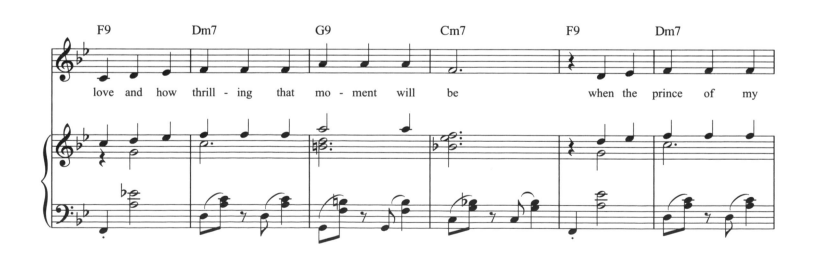

Sweet Georgia Brown

Words and Music by Ben Bernie, Maceo Pinkard and Kenneth Casey

No gal made has got a shade__ on Sweet Geor-gia Brown.__

Two left feet, but oh so neat__ has Sweet Geor-gia Brown.__

84

D.S. al Coda

Coda

Take The "A" Train

Words and Music by Billy Strayhorn

There Is No Greater Love

Words and Music by Marty Symes and Isham Jones

Unforgettable

Words and Music by Irving Gordon

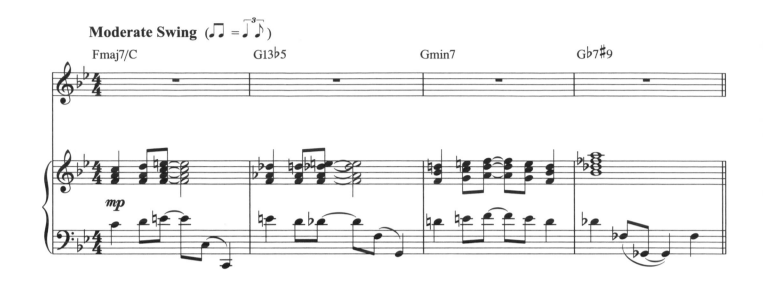

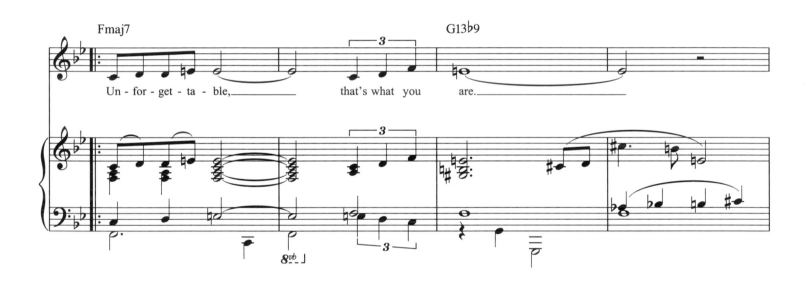

Like a song of love that clings_ to me, how the thought of you does things_ to me.

Nev - er be - fore____ has some - one been more____

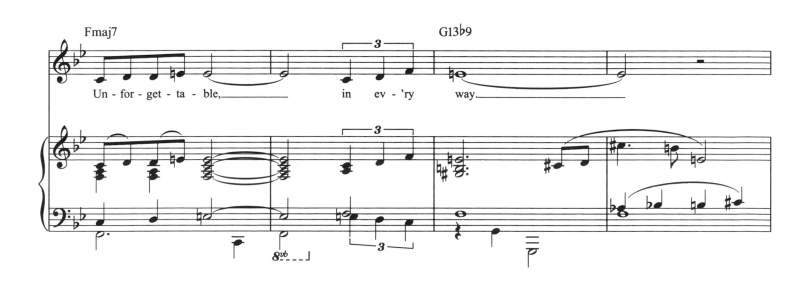

Un - for - get - ta - ble,____ in ev - 'ry way.____